# CHAPTERS


INTRODUCTION
1.    WHO AM I?
2.    THINKING RIGHT
3.    THE RIGHT PEOPLE ON THE BUS
4.    ORGANIZATIONAL STRUCTURE
5.    SONG CHOICE
6.    CONNECTING OFF STAGE
7.    CONNECTING ON STAGE
8.    IMAGE
9.    WEBSITE / PRESS KIT
10.    PROMOTIONAL VIDEO
11.    BOOKINGYOURBAND
12.    BOOKINGAGENTS
13.    MANAGER ROAD MANAGER
14.    FOLLOW UP
15.    STAYING ORGANIZED
16.    SOUND AND LIGHT PRODUCTION
17.    THE CREW
18.    SOCIAL MEDIA
19.    EMAIL LIST
20.    CONCLUSION

## Introduction

American Idol has done a lot of interesting things for this industry. Whether you like it or not, it has had a major impact. One of the things I find extremely fascinating is the number of people that said this was their life long dream to be a singer and they clearly did not have what it takes vocally. So who is wrong, the singer wanna be or Simon?

I don't know what reason led to that person thinking singing was their deal but I would

imagine they didn't qualify it with a few key elements. See...when something is your thing, passion dream, etc, you will do everything you can to spend time perfecting it. You will want to do that work for hours because you enjoy it. Time disappears for you when you are spending time in your zone of genius. This is how I made the decision to turn all lead vocals in a group I started as the lead singer over to my brother. I recognized that every time I went into my studio to work on getting better, I would always grab the guitar and not the microphone. And sure enough the next 3-4 hours would disappear. I also began to realize as I was recording myself a hundred times on any given song, I was never happy with what I heard back. The final straw for me came after listening back to a one time rough take my brother recorded and realizing that this was clearly his deal. And of course it is.
He lived with us a number of years ago when he moved back from Texas until he got his own place. We had 5 acres of trees that he would wander thru with his guitar singing for hours.
There is a lot of work to be done to have a successful music career, so if you haven't figured out that music on any level is or isn't in

your zone of genius, then that is the first step. No one including yourself can market a successful career on a half in decision or passion. It's a waste of everyone's time, mostly yours.

Now if you absolutely love music, but are realizing you may have missed your mark on what role you can play, don't let that stop you from exploring other options. We have a girl working for us now that has been passionate about music her whole life. You can see it all over her face at concerts. She is thoroughly living in the moment. Another thing she is really good at and enjoys doing is cold calling and working with people. Put those two passions together and it makes for a special kind of opportunity that will allow her to live out her life doing what she loves.

Hopefully you are beginning to get the point. The discovery of your "zone of genius" can appear to happen almost accidentally at times, but mark my words, it's no accident. It comes from that moment in our lives when we are open enough to allow the message to get through. Learn to cultivate that openness and not only will your path to genius become clearer and more frequent, but the pieces will fall in place quicker too.

**Why should you continue reading and what do we know?**

My brother and I have collectively spent a great amount of time in virtually every aspect that it takes to run a successful and financially viable music career. Here is a list of our some of our experiences below:

- Own a book agency
- Owned a marketing and advertising company
- Own a video production company
- Professional live sound engineer
- Professional recording engineer
- Website Development
- Traveled for years playing music professionally
- Shared the stage with many, many national artists

And best of all, we were our own first customer to make sure we had what it takes to teach you. Everything in this program we have done and are doing today for our own group, Big Time Grain Co. We get paid more than most regional acts and as even as much as some up and coming national label acts. We've done this all with no record label, no major radio support, and no external booking agency or management. We choose our own schedule and we are free to write the songs we want. Our training program, although geared mostly towards music, has the power to help anyone, in any career, whether connected to music or not. This world has become so exciting for those who choose to open their minds to the possibilities. We look forward to cultivating your story of genius and success.

# 1. Who am I...

and why should you listen to me or anything written in the following chapters? My name is Chad Bourquin and my brother/partner is Bret Bourquin. Together, besides being brothers, we make up the duo of Big Time Grain Co. (https://www.bigtimegrain.com) There is a decent chance you may be saying to yourself, who is Big Time Grain Co., and why would I listen to someone I've never heard of? Great question and the answer is simple. The reason the information in the following videos is so valid is because we have accomplished on some level what it was that caused you to get this book to begin with. And we have done so without the aid of record label support, radio support and all of the other traditional music industry paths of the past.

We have learned to make money doing what we love while growing a methodical business structure that we will teach to you in the following chapters. Should you decide to take it further, there is a complete video training program available as well. We maintain total creative control of our music. We have a road crew, a support staff and play really cool gigs for great money. Most of the success written about here took place within the first five years.

Part of the reason we accomplished our success in such a short time is because this was not our first rodeo. Collectively, we bring years of making many mistakes in multiple groups.  Our growth from these mistakes eventually allowed us to grow and learn what we needed to ultimately overcome them.  Our goal now is to help you learn and benefit from everything we've learned. Imagine if you could jump over those mistakes to expedite your career. How cool would that be?

Don't rush through this process. If you are driven only by the end result, this will get overwhelming fast and you will miss some of the best experiences of your life in developing your music career. The whole process should be fun, after all you are working on something you love, right? Granted, not all of the pieces will be in your wheelhouse and just come naturally, but they are all doable and achievable. Eat this elephant one bite at a time and you will turn around one day and be amazed at how far you have come.

For the most part, it's important to read these chapters in order. Many of them will build on lessons from previous chapters. Even if you have a head start on certain topics, it can be the finite little subtleties that make all the difference. So many times in my life and music career, it was these little shifts that made the biggest difference for me. Read and re-read. If needed, then re-read again. This is your dream, remember? It's worth it.

Record label vs independent. To be clear, we are not saying a record label isn't in your future. What we are saying is that if you are going to get a record deal, you have a better chance at getting their interest and holding more chips at the bargaining table, if you have applied the principles consistently in this program. It's like the guy that already has a girlfriend who seems to end up with more opportunities for other girlfriends than when he was single. Why, because he is confident in where he is at in life and that is attractive to others. If your music career is going to thrive on any level, you are going to lose the needy vibe you may be putting off now, repelling everyone around you. Worst case scenario, or in our opinion, maybe best case scenario, you spend the rest of your music career independent, calling your own shots, creating the music you want, with a fan base following you because they love what you are doing. The best part, you'll love it too.  Buckle up, it's time to start living the rest of your creative life. Let's have some fun.

# 2. Thinking Right

The reality is that some of you will skip over this section due to you feeling a lack of importance in it. Why not, I always skipped these sections when I didn't know better too. I was always about getting to what I considered to be the result producing activity right away, so I could get the quickest possible results. Here is the absolute truth. I had to learn and am still learning the content on this section. Had I learned it first, the success I achieved because of it could have happened way earlier. It was up to me.

Our thoughts decide our future. Think about all the times you have thought something positive or negative and it came true somewhere down the line. Think about the times you just thought of someone you hadn't seen in awhile and they either called you, you ran into them or you called them and they said I was just thinking about you. You might be asking, what about all the thoughts that I have that don't come true? Well here is the cold hard answer. Those things are on their way to you bar one big caveat. What kind of resistance are you countering them with? Are you thinking about some specific success with your music, but then turning around and complaining to a friend about your current lack of success? You can't have both. Either you believe you are going to succeed at this music thing or you don't. Are you talking about your music in a successful tone, but talking negative about other people? Are you looking at other people's success with a feeling of envy? I can go on and on giving you self defeating scenarios like this and still not hit all the ways you may self sabotage your own success.
It is impossible to hyper analyze every thought, but what we can do is get better at paying attention to how each thought makes us feel.

How we feel can be used as our internal guidance system to let us know how we are doing. The more we use it, the better we get at recognizing it. You may say or think something today that doesn't even register, but a month down the road that same thought rings the guidance system like a bell. This will be life changing to you in all areas of your life and is the biggest key to you reaching your goals in your music career.

Just from a simple performance prospective, this business is all about connecting to people, on and off stage. When you go to a concert and the artist has something going on that's a little funky, your subconscious picks up on it even if you consciously don't. By contrast, if the artist has done the work I've referred to above, you can find yourself liking the artist, even supporting the artist whether you like their music or not.

Like it or not, you are in a field of sales here. Authentic pure thinking can move people to great lengths. That's what you want your music to do right?

Mark my words, the people that succeed the most with this program, either have already begun this process of learning right thinking or they began it here and never stopped.

You won't ever get there, you will just keep getting better. So why is this such a big deal? It's simple. Do you want to build your music career with a sledge hammer and tons of sweat and tears or do you want to learn how to attract success to you. You may get there with option one, but it will come at a much greater cost. The second option is way more fun and most definitely more effective. I have personally watched hundreds of videos and read lots of books on this to get where I am today. This one chapter here is not enough to make the kind of changes you need to, but hopefully it is the beginning prod you need to move to the next step. You can't spend too much time on this subject and it's important to learn from others as well. Here is a link to a blog that will go deeper for you on these topics.

https://www.playmusicmakemore.com/blog

# 3. The Right People on the Tour Bus

The foundation is the key to all successful organizations. The book "Good to Great" puts a huge emphasis on having the right people on the bus. This especially applies to you if you have aspirations of traveling to shows on a bus. Lester Estelle Jr. https://www.dreambigseries.com/lester-estelle-jr  was in Nashville for only 6 months before Big and Rich hired him. Nashville is known for being a 6-7 year town to get yourself known and integrated. Not for Lester. People that didn't know Lester, found out quickly that not only could he play with the best of them, but he is just flat out a good dude. Bands at the highest levels won't tolerate bad attitudes, so why should you. If you don't look forward to hanging out with every member you have in your band, whether you are playing or not, fix that immediately.

You are not responsible for fixing someone else's bad attitude, but when that bad attitude goes south at a gig, you are responsible for that. There is much work to do throughout this program. Release the anchors immediately.

If you hire correctly from the beginning, you most likely won't have to deal with problems like this on the back end. Do your research on everyone you hire. Get references and not just music ones. Mostly, if your gut starts twisting in the slightest, pay attention. Don't let your huge desire for a successful music career cloud your vision. If you are the type of person that sees the best in people, congratulations, that is a fantastic character trait.   However, you do need to recognize it and get outside opinions to help make these decisions.

When I mentioned at the beginning of the book that we can help you miss some potholes, this is a big one. Not only did we spend too much time in this hole, we rented a dredger and dug it deeper.

Make a commitment to yourself that you will give character and talent equal portions in your decision making. In spite of our rapid growth, I can clearly link stagnant growth to bad hiring decisions first and taking too long to cut the ties second. I can also link revitalized growth to moving past those situations. Don't hold grudges or take it personal. Just learn from it. Here are some questions to ask when interviewing a potential band or crew member.

1. What are you doing to get better as a musician? (If they don't have an answer.. .red flag )

2. What are you doing to better yourself as a person? (This one might get you a raised eyebrow, but ask it anyway. It's important. )
3. What was the last band you were in?
4. Why are you not in that band any more? (Negative, blaming type answers will be a red flag .)

You will surely have other questions that will fit more specifically into what you are looking for, but the ones above can save you a lot of time and potential grief.

Other things to look at are gear. Is it kept up? If a guitar player has a pedal board, how organized is the pedalboard? You can have some latitude here, but a messy pedalboard can be signs of a messy life.

Also, look for responses that might contain any drama in them. People who talk about drama, attract drama. FYI, if you only seem to be getting inquiries from this type of candidate, it might be good to spend a little introspective time yourself. We noticed that when we got better as a people, we attracted better. Just a thought.

This philosophy applies to band members for sure, but becomes even more crucial when you are moving to hiring managers, agents and others that will be the face of your group with first impressions. As artists, we just want to play our music, so we can be very susceptible to flashy words and promises in hopes of releasing all the work we don't want to do. The right people will be genuinely interested in your success without ulterior motives. Yes they will want paid of course, but that will be the extent of their ulterior motives. Pay attention to speech, eye contact, mannerisms and posture and again...get 2nd, 3rd, 4th and 5th opinions.

Now that we are on the backside of this lesson, let me tell you the differences we experience with our group. We laugh a lot. We help each other through challenges. We coexist and get along in smaller areas.  Most importantly, when we walk on stage, there is genuine appreciation throughout the group for each other as people first and talented musicians second. This is worth every bit of time and attention you put into it.

# 4. Organizational Structure

Setting up your organizational and pay structure correctly from the beginning can be the difference between you and your band all being on the same page or there being discord among the ranks. The "we are a band" concept works as long as there are equal shares in duties that match an equal share in pay. This, more often than not, is not the case. If it is, congrats and keep going. There is huge power and benefit from 4-5 members all being on the same page and all working towards a common goal. It can be a great experience for everyone. That being said, this is an extremely rare situation that very few groups have. Most of the time, you have one or maybe two band members doing a bulk of the non-musical work and taking an equal cut as the rest of the band. Of course the rest of the band is fine with this scenario. However, the member or members that are doing the work will at some point begin to resent the other members due to an imbalance of work versus pay. This resentment will continue to fester until at some point it comes to a head of frustration.

Another imbalance can be caused from an investment point of view. Example: One member buys all the sound production, lights, etc and yet still takes the same cut as the rest of the band at shows. This adds to tension when the band member bankrolling the operation wants to advance the career by investing more into it with no buy in from the other members who are content with the way things are. I doubt there is another industry on the planet that allows this to happen. In fact, most successful business owners would describe a practice like this as ludicrous.

Here are some solutions. Figure out some sort of percentage split that accounts for effort = reward or investment = reward. This is not the best plan since you are still giving decision making power to members that may or may not want to grow with the project. Remember, you started reading this because you wanted to take control of your musical career. Why on earth would you decide you want to do that and then relinquish it to unwilling parties?

Here is what I consider the best solution. You own the business yourself. Or in the case of my brother and I, you have an equal partnership with someone you have a long standing, proven, tested and equal relationship with. My brother and I have been brothers our whole lives. We know more about each other than just about anyone else in the world. Before you partner up, you and your partner's relationship shouldn't be too much short of that.

We own the sound, the lights, the bus, the trailer and more. We do all the marketing, planning, booking, repairs etc. We pay for new gear, new tires, album recordings, videos, on and on. You get the point. We pay our band members flat rates which is equal to or better than most hired gun musicians out of Nashville. We pay additional wages on travel dates that are overnight without a show the next day. We make sure at least one meal per day is taken care of on almost all shows, especially if travel is involved. We normally get that covered by the purchaser. Nashville hired gun rates are $150 - $250 per show with a $75 - $100 travel day rate. You may not be able to start as high of rate as you want for your band members and that's ok. Just be fair while still being able to keep the business operational and growing.

Bottom line, we love our guys and we do everything we can to make sure they feel valued and taken care of. With that, we also value their opinions and try to regularly ask for those opinions. That all being said, the buck stops with my brother and I. If we need to make a quick decision, it doesn't require a board meeting with a vote that may or may not get pushed through. Of course, our wrong decisions also come out of our pockets and our pockets alone. But here's what we've learned. Successful people make decisions quickly and listen to their intuition on whether or not to make that decision. This becomes way more challenging when deciding by committee. Again, there are exceptions to this rule. Just make sure you're one of them before you go down that path.

You are in the driver's seat. You are not perfect, so when you make mistakes, own up to them quickly. Apologize for the ones that affect your band or crew members. Communicate your vision often without exaggeration. Use sentences like, "this is what we are working on" or "we are going for this goal" as opposed to predicting how and when successes are going to happen. Dogmatic predictions will catch up to you and eventually cause wavering among the troops. Give your band members the confidence in your ability to make decisive decisions. Let them see you steer the bus with confidence.

# 5. Song Choice

Song choice can make or break your band. When talking about covers, you have to decide if you are more concerned about your own musical freedoms or what your fans and crowd want to hear. Before we go into this, here is what we are not saying you should do. I am not asking you to play songs you can't stand or that you have trouble connecting with no matter how popular the song is. I am also not saying you have to play the songs exactly like they were recorded for them to be accepted. One exception to that is if you are trying to make your mark as a tribute band. Then yes, you must get as close as possible because that is what the buyer is purchasing. On the flip side, if you are not a tribute band then putting your own spin on songs is recommended. The more you try to sound just like the original, the more you will be compared to the original. Think back to the American Idol or Voice performances that stood out the most. It was most likely the versions the artist made their own that were the most memorable for you. Back to song selections. Pick songs that people know. I know some artists that try to be different by selecting the non-hits off the artist album. If you are old enough to remember 45 records, it would be the equivalent to the b side. This path of originality will cap your growth as an artist. A much more effective path is to pick songs that people know and love and express your creativity in making it your own. Make sure to maintain the integrity of the melody and hook line in the process, but make it fun. Explore different ideas within the song to put your mark on it. Most importantly, capitalize on your strengths within the song. This is how you begin to create moments in your shows that people connect with and remember.

Tom Jackson's book "Live Music Method" is the best book we know about on the market for helping you do this. This book goes for $80 - $100 a copy based on digital or hard copy. That sounds expensive for a book, but when you factor in that he gets  somewhere around $1000 per day to coach artists with this material, the price is minimal. If you increase your value as an artist, your pay will follow suit.

There are so many nuggets in Tom's book that make it worth the money and would warrant you purchasing it. One of the key ideas he will give you is to rate your songs based on energy level from 1-5 with 5 being the most energy to 1 being the least. If your show is multiple sets, treat each set like it's own show. You start your set at 4, work your way to a 1 in the middle of the show and then climb back to a 5 for the end of the show or set. This is a gross generalization of a book full of ways to improve your show. Creating moments in shows is a big step towards growing true fans and bigger crowds. In his book, Tom leads you through the steps to categorize your songs based on energy level and how to place those songs in the perfect order that will lead your crowds on a journey of emotion and eating out of the palm of your hand. This business is about connecting to fans. That starts with proper song selection as well as correct song placement. Your ego can have a tendency to cause you problems here if you allow it to. Go ahead and throw your ego in the trash and put your fans and future fans first.

Song selection becomes even more important if you have a desire to play your original music in the same shows you were hired to play your cover tunes at. You can successfully sneak in your originals to your set if you do so sparingly and you actually do sneak them in. It's very helpful to know your venue's expectations in this area. If the expectations are cover songs, don't give your originals a big introduction with a spot light. Pick your originals that people can dance to whether slow or fast and of course place them at the correct spots on the energy scale that Tom talks about. The more popular the cover songs you pick, the more tolerance there will be for your original placement. As you gain popularity, you will also gain increased tolerance from venue owners and increased expectations from fans to play your originals. As this happens, it is completely ok and even a good idea to begin setting up some of your originals with stories that can help your fans connect to them. There are occasions you can do this early on, just know your venue.

A note to all original bands. If you are dead set on not doing covers, there are still many parts of this training that will help you reach your goals. If that is the case, you do need to be realistic about the pay rates for all original groups. As you probably already know, the bulk of your shows consist of club dates that involve 2-3 other bands where everyone splits the door after you pay the sound man. Also, don't quit your day job. This is not meant to discourage you at all. Just be realistic if you choose this path. The younger you are, the easier this method is if you don't have a mortgage, wife and kids. At some point in my career, I figured out that I was getting to play 5-9 original songs in those 3-4 band gigs and barely paying for the gas. I also figured out, I could learn popular covers, get hired for 3-4 hour gigs and filter in those same 5-9 original songs to a new crowd every show and make decent money. I love to play music. If making a decision like this was going to allow me to do that more, for more money, while increasing my fan base, it was a no brainer.

# 6. Connecting Off Stage

Touch a heart before asking for a hand. People go to concerts to be moved. They become fans and even true fans of artists that do that for them consistently.

As artists, you probably recognized early on and even learned to enjoy the exchange of energy that happens between you and the audience when you accomplish an energizing connection. This is an important subject and there are a lot of ideas here. Don't let it overwhelm you, just pick the ones that you connect with the most right now and start there. When you feel you have mastered that, move on to the next one while continuing to apply all the previous ones.

In the beginning stages of your career, you will have many opportunities for off stage connecting. This is the pre-show, break and post-show. This is where you work the room, meeting new people and thanking the returning fans for choosing to spend their valuable time with you. So many artists, present company included, are introverts. This is not easy for us to do. We really would rather go crawl in the corner and re-energize ourselves.

But that is not an option for the artist that wants to grow. We have to suck it up and find ways to enjoy this part of it. Here is what works for me. I make it a learning expedition. How many interesting things can I learn about the people in our audience? Also, how many ways can I make them feel good about choosing to spend this time with us? Here's a big one. How

much can I help them to feel included in our journey? Everyone wants to feel included and we all look for ways to do that. We also all want to be part of something bigger than ourselves. You figure out how to let your fans be part of your big picture, and you are on the path to gold. The simplest way to put this is, just be interested in them as people.
Helpful hints:
There is a balance between spending enough quality time with any given person and not allowing your entire time to be consumed by one person when there are many more in the crowd hoping for the same thing. To navigate this, be fully engaged with the person you are talking with while you are talking with them. Once you feel a natural break in the conversation, tell them it was great talking with them and let them know there are a few more people you need to chat with before you get back on stage or leave or whatever the case is.
**That one fan** . We all usually have one of these that will attempt to consume every bit of non-stage time you have. This fan usually doesn't breathe between sentences and so there is no natural break in the conversation.
 But yet, they are always there supporting your

cause.  First off, always maintain a feeling of gratitude for this person. You may be the only thing keeping them from going over the edge. We don't always get the full picture of the impact we have on people. However, you may have to get good at breaking the conversation with a bit more assertiveness. It's ok, just do it gracefully and show gratitude for them showing up to your show. With that being said, if your gut tells you to keep talking to that person at that particular time, listen to your gut.

Teach your bandmates why it's important for them to learn these skills as well. Help them understand that if the success of the band increases, so do the dollars and amount of gigs for everyone. Also, help them to grasp that this is a big step towards advancing their own career as well. Sometimes, their tendency can be to think, "I'm just a hired gun, why do I need to help advance the band?" If your band is thinking that way, it may be time to revisit casting the vision. As long as you have the right people on the bus, this is usually just an educational issue.

**Connecting with the people that hired you.**
We will spend more time on this in the "Booking your band" section but for now let's

talk about connecting with the purchaser, bar manager, staff, etc. You have one chance to make a first impression. Make it a priority to greet anyone connected with the venue with a smile and treat all of them, including the cleaning crew, with the utmost respect. They all can be your friend and ally in your growth as a band. I had a conversation the following morning of a concert with the cleaning crew for a few minutes before we headed out when one of them mentioned, "we usually don't have to clean this much after a Thursday night, but every table in this place was dirty." Now, tell me you see value in that information that I would have never known had I not treated the cleaning crew with respect and kindness. Also, always tip the wait and bar staff if they served you. You are not excluded because you are the help. What do you think the staff will say when the owner asks them their opinion on which bands they like the best?

The bottom line of this section...be a nice person.

# 7. Connecting On Stage

To truly connect with your audience, there are certainly some techniques, but before we get into those, we have to cover the most important part of that process. Are you the artist connected to the song? You might be thinking, "this is a lead singer issue and doesn't involve anyone else".  That is so far from the truth. Every musician on stage, if serious about making their mark on their audience must devote some time to mastering this skill. That begins with connecting with each song and that begins with clearing your mind of anything else that will keep you from connecting with the song. This can be difficult at first when there is usually a lot going on around you pulling your mental attention away. Here are some examples:

- Someone is trying to get your attention to make a request
- Some girl thinks you're cute and is working hard to distract you
- An entire table gets up and leaves and you start to think it's because of you.

If you are not mentally prepared, all these and more will impact your show and not in a good way.

Your audience wants to feel something and you my friend are the conduit to get them there. You do that by connecting to not only each song independently, but each moment in each song. Learning to be fully present while still maintaining an awareness around you is its own art form.

One of our teachers used to talk about hitting a mental reset button at the end of each song. He would indicate that literally by taking his finger and pushing an imaginary button on the other arm. This was to signify that the previous song was over. Every moment that happened or didn't happen in that song was gone, never to be experienced again.

Don't wait for showtime to practice this. Practice it during your band rehearsal, as well as your own private practice time. Visualize yourself on a big stage with a huge audience. Imagine the lights are in your face, the sound is pumping and you are embracing each moment of the song you are working on as your imaginary crowd feeds off your energy and passion. Do this until you feel you are able to get into the moment instantly. Don't feel bad if you can't make it happen on a particular song. Just get rid of that song. There are too many great songs out there for you to have to struggle with connecting to that one. Whether the struggle is lyrical, melodic or just overall feel, send it hiking.

One technique to help you connect with your audience is called "painting the room." Have you ever been to a concert or show where you feel one side of the room is getting all of the attention and it is not your side?  You may be doing this without even realizing it. Learn to paint the room by having eye contact with the different sections of the entire room, even if you can't actually see their eyes. Cover the front left, the back left, the front center, the balcony left...well, you get the picture. Hold your eye contact long enough to feel a connection, but not so long that it becomes creepy. You will get a better feel for this the more you do it. What you don't want to do is bounce your eye contact around too quickly. That can cause a nervous tension in the room. Also, pay close attention to how much you keep your eyes closed. It's completely fine for effect, but if it's happening for other reasons like habit or you are using it to feel safe, then it's not ok. In fact, the eyes are the window to the soul. Keeping your eyes closed too much is like training for years then putting on leg weights for the big race.

Body position is equally as important. In sales training you are taught to never cross your legs away from your client or cross your arms so not to close yourself off from them. It's the same thing here. There are moments where it is cool for impact to turn and face another band member to engage in a jam. That practice is good and should be done with each band member throughout a show. With that being said, if you are in the middle of singing lyrics, avoid turning and singing to the drummer. If the drummer is doing a solo, it's absolutely cool and recommended to turn and put the focus on the drummer or any other solo section. The main idea here is, keep your body position open to your audience most of the time.

Another concept for the whole band to learn is stage placement. If a hole opens up on the stage, a band member should move to that spot. Done perfectly, this happens the whole show. This allows each band member to spend time in each section of the stage, painting the room from each vantage point.

I can hear your mental conflict saying, "Wait a minute, in the first part of the section you talked about connecting with each moment in each song and now you're giving all these techniques and tasks to do at the same time." You are correct. It is impossible to properly connect to a song if you don't know that song like the back of your hand. That comes from pure repetition of your gifts and skills so that you no longer have to think about remembering lyrics or chords. It is the same thing with these techniques. Practice them to the point you don't have to think about them anymore and they are happening instinctively and naturally.

As mentioned in the **Off Stage Connecting** section, Tom Jackson wrote an amazing book called the "Live Music Method" with much more detail on how to make your stage show look like the pros.

# 8. Image

Figuring out your artist / band image is the first step to getting your marketing material right. Who are you? What do you believe? What do you look like? What do you sound like? The quickest and easiest way to figure out your image is to research all the groups that have influenced you along the way and bands/artists that you really like. Like parenting, these artists all played roles in your musical growth and therefore can be helpful in figuring out your image. Once you have your list of 5 - 10 artists, begin to look for commonalities among them, no matter how subtle they may be. This exercise is simply to give you a deeper look into yourself. Also began to look at which of these groups seem to have the most pull on you by just looking at their website and pictures. What is it about the pictures you like the most?

*Warning:* As you are developing your image and identifying which beliefs you want to be included in your image, make sure you understand the ramifications of each belief you are about to hang your hat on before you do it. The biggest example of this would be politics. If you live in the U.S., you know how polarized our country currently is. People are changing their support of artists simply because of conflicting political beliefs. If you feel it is part of your life mission to hold a flag for one side or the other, you must be alright with the fact you just essentially cut your U.S. market in half for potential fans. More than that, you have decreased the number of people that will hire you even more because they don't want to take sides for their own business sake no matter which side they are personally on. I book a lot of bands and have seen this play out in real life many times which is why this discussion warrants some time on it. If you are as big as U2 or Toby Keith, you have some financial latitude and can make decisions differently if you want. That's obviously not the case since you are reading this, so be smart. Things to notice about your favorite artists. What do they wear? What style of pictures do they take? What kind of songs do they write? Is any of it similar to you? There is a book out there called "Steal Like An Artist". It's a great little, easy read with lots of pictures and the overall message is, nothing under the sun is completely original, but our originality comes from our own collaborations of other artist's material. This applies to image too. Discover the parts you like best about images of other artists, make it your own and then own it.

**Promo pictures:** I have personally built a number of websites over the years and learned something big out of that process. Great pictures, make great looking websites. Without great pictures, you're polishing a turd.

Do some searches in your town and find the best BAND/ARTIST photographer in town. Then, pay what they want for a photo shoot. This is not necessary for you to keep playing low level bar gigs, but if you want to break out of that, this is the first place to spend money. When we started Big Time Grain Co, we had years of bad photo experiences under our belts with other bands. We made sure our look was bigger than we were. Even though our pictures are way better now then when we started, they were still good at that time too. Before anyone had ever heard us, we booked 7 gigs at a higher pay, then my previous group of 15 years was making. How??? Image, image, image. Now, to be fair, we actually had to perform well at those 7 gigs to keep going, but that is what image can do for you. Any chance you can improve your image, do it. Just make sure that you maintain some consistency so your brand doesn't confuse your audience.

If you are going to make a big shift at some point, be sure about it, then do it methodically with confidence.

Here are some examples of pictures a photographer of ours has taken that captures the essence of what people can expect at our shows. As you look at them, see if you can't get an idea of the vibe that happens at the show just from looking at the pictures. BTGC - Gallery

# 9. Website / Press Kit

One of the questions I get asked the most often from bands is, "Do I need a website, or can I just use Facebook?"
Hopefully after going through the section on Image this answer is already clear to you. Pros have websites, amateurs use Facebook for their website. We also discussed in that section how important great promo photos are to a great looking website. Companies like Wix, Square, Bandzoogle and more have made it so easy to put together great looking websites, that you almost just need to use one of their templates. Then you just replace it with your info and images. Our website was built with Wix and personally find it the easiest to work with but you may find the other platforms better for you. If budget is not a concern to you, then you can hire this done by a pro and save yourself time that you can be applying

elsewhere. You are probably looking at between $1000 to $5000 on the top end. Just make sure you have given the developer some very clear examples of what you like and make sure they have a great understanding of the optimization process. Also, make sure that they are doing this on a platform that you can easily make small edits to with new pics, videos, songs, if you don't want to be paying and relying on someone else every time that needs done. Before you get started, spend some time looking at your favorite artist's website for ideas. Did I mention, great pictures will make this much easier?

**Website vs Press Kit.** Both of these are needed and both serve completely different purposes. Your website is for your fans and your press kit should be designed to get you gigs. Your press kit can be one of the pages on your website if you want.

**Website:** Your front page should be all about first impressions, fan collection for email list and social media. It should have a great picture, a video of one of your songs if you have it, some kind of collection form for your email list and link to all your social media accounts. The best thing you can put on your front page is a short video helping the fan to get to know a little about who you are and what you are all about. Other pages can include a photo gallery, more videos, about or bio section, music or media, schedule or tour and contact. Most website templates are making this easy now, but make sure you pay attention to the mobile view editing as well. Google is penalizing websites that are not paying attention to this and are not pleasing to the eye on a mobile phone. Plus, most people are going to be looking at it on their phone anyway.

**Optimization:** Companies like Wix have made this easy. They virtually lead you through the optimization process one step at a time. I always try to ask potential clients how they heard about the group, and if they didn't already know who we were, many times it was because we popped up at the top on a google search.

**Press kit:** This is all about what the buyer will want to know about your band. We will talk about a promo video later but once you have one, the video should be at the top directly under the promo picture. Your booking contact info should be at the top right and easy to find and access. Down the page, place a short bio along with a few testimonies with a link to read more. As you get bookings with clients that have recognizable names, put together an image with their logos on it titled past clients. As long as your schedule has dates on it, you can put that on the press kit as well.

**Schedule:** Currently, one of the easiest schedule formats is Bandsintown.com. Not only can you develop a following on their platform, but they also easily integrate with Facebook and have embedded code that will work with most websites. As a DIY musician, efficiency will be your best friend. Redundancy in your efforts won't.

**URL:** Find a good website .com url that will be easy for people to remember.

**Email:** Get at least one email that uses your website url in it so you are not sending and receiving booking and business emails from Gmail, Yahoo or something like that. Create an automatic signature in that email with your name, phone number and website when you have it. You can include a couple social links too.

Sincerely,

Here is an example.

Chad Bourquin

(913) 238-0151 | booking@bigtimegrain.com | Bigtimegrain.com

# 10. Promotional Video

Of all the marketing efforts we have done, the video promo single handedly has done more work for us in getting quality, high paying shows then anything we have done. Stating the obvious again, you still want to make sure your band and performance is rock solid before doing this, but if you have done that work, this can catapult you quickly if done correctly. These are so important, we have continued to do new videos and have updated it at least 4 times as the band has gotten better.

This is strictly a promo video to get you more high paying jobs. It is all about picking 5 of your best covers and getting a quality audio and video capture of 30-45 seconds sections of each one. In picking the songs, think about which ones you get the most compliments on to help you narrow this down. Also, think about the flow of energy. It should look similar to this on a 1-5 energy scale with 5 being the most energetic.

Song 1 - Energy 4

Song 2 - Energy 3-4
Song 3 - Energy 1-2
Song 4 - Energy 3-4
Song 5 - Energy 5
Pick songs that fit in the lead vocalist sweet spot and try to pick at least 10 to capture. If you get the whole night captured that's fine, but keep in mind that someone is going to have to go through all that footage and if you are paying for this, that can increase your bill. Way out in front of the shoot, if you haven't done this already, start to work with your group helping them be aware of facial expressions and to be conscious about smiling, unless of course you are a death metal band. I have booked other artists where the buyer said he bought them because he liked their smile. That artist was not the strongest of the 3 options I gave the buyer to pick from. People want an experience and they want to have fun. Print off white sheets of paper that say smile and put them under every mic stand until this becomes a habit, preferably before the shoot.

**Location:** The perfect location for this will be a venue or event that already has a professional sound and lighting rig with a built in crowd. We've done ours mostly in the evening slots at festivals. The goal is to look bigger than life in the videos and the venue can certainly help. However, I have seen some really well done videos without the built in crowd. The band just made sure to keep all of the camera shots and angles really close and tight. Even if you have to book a show where you know you aren't going to make any money but it's a killer venue, do it. The rewards and pay off down the road will more than make up for it.

**Audio:** This is equally as important as the video quality. Many of the pro sound boards out today allow for live multi tracking. This is what you want. You want to have the ability to mix this separately after the event with the option to fix something if needed. If you are planning to do this at an existing event, make sure to communicate first with the promoter, getting permission and with the sound company to ask for their help in capturing the audio. Be willing to pay the engineer for the additional effort in this process. Probably $50-$200.

After our first promo video for this group, it seemed like we went up $1000 in our rate almost overnight. It has gotten easier and easier to increase our rate with each new video we have done with a little bit better quality of production and performance. I was recently on the phone with someone who had never heard of us that thought I was going to quote 2-3 times what I did based on what he saw in our video.

**Additional Video Items:** Put a less than 5 second header with your logo on it. In the bumper make sure to include contact info for booking. Text based testimonies are good to add in throughout the video. Some people will add in some interview type clips throughout.  This is OK as long as it's extremely short and doesn't drag out. Keep in mind that most buyers are going thru multiple videos and promos and the last thing you want them to do is quit watching due to an extended interview in the promo.  In my opinion, these styles of videos are more for the fans and that is a completely different video.
Example:  *https://www.bigtimegrain.com/epk*

# 11. Booking your band

Alright, be honest. Did you skip over most of the previous sections to get to this one? Ask me how I know? Because most of my life that is exactly what I would have done. I would have thought, yea, yea, yea...give me the action steps so I can get on with it. Unfortunately, if this is your approach you will miss many valuable insights that build on each other and will ultimately lead to the success of booking your band. My hope is, if you are like my old self, stop now and go back to the beginning. For the rest of you, onward upward. If you are completely confident in your band (the product) after going through the previous sections, it's time to talk about booking more and better gigs? First off, know that if you have done the work, the gigs will come to you to the extent of how much attention you have paid to all those previous items. Let me put on my agent hat for a bit. I have been an agent for over 15 years. I send out almost 100 1099 forms to bands every year. A few of my purchasing clients, which are major shopping centers in town, redirect every band inquiry they get to me. What that means to you, is I have definitely learned what successful bands do to get my attention and also what doesn't work. There is a direct correlation between bands that need the most improving and how over the top their sales pitch and neediness is. The bands we work with that make the most money, the kind of money you want to make, never, and I mean never call me to get more gigs. I call them, because the client is always requesting them. Why...they have done the work.

I apologize if you were looking for a magical pitch here, but there isn't one. There are some basic people skills that can be very helpful. Also, I am not saying you should sit in your basement and wait for the calls to come in if you are starting out. That won't happen. It is basic supply and demand. If you are new, and need the experience, go play every chance you can. Even if there is little or no pay. If this is where you are at, make sure you are working on the skills, especially in the "Connecting on Stage" and "Connecting Off Stage" sections. As your demand goes up, raise your price with it incrementally.

People skills are a necessity for booking your band. On the phone, pay attention to your facial expression. A smile on your end will help the person on the other end feel more comfortable. Let the person on the other end talk more and you listen more. You do this with answering questions of theirs with questions of yours before getting to the answer. This not only helps them feel you care about making sure you are the right fit, but it also helps you to have all the facts before answering. An example of this is when they ask you how much your band rate is, respond with "We have created packages to help with this that involve different numbers of band members as well as different sizes of production with extra bells and whistles." So here are some questions I ask when asked about price. "Is production (sound and lights) provided? Is there a stage? What time do you want the concert to start and end? Are you looking for a large band performance or more of a broken down acoustic show? What do you expect your attendance to be like? Are you selling tickets or is this a free event?"

Usually my last question after some or all of these questions is "do you have a budget range you want to be within?"

Let the conversation flow naturally. Don't force a question and if the buyer pushes the rate area right out of the gate, give them your range. Then explain to them that the range is based on how many band members, how long the show is, production requirements, etc. In no way am I attempting to avoid the question or skate telling them our price.

That's why we created packages, so that we have the ability to work within multiple budgets and still make it viable. Make your packages realistic for where you currently fit in the market and where the demand for your band is. Be careful not to over do the packages, especially in the beginning. You don't want to come off pretentious. The absolute bottom line on this is, the better you do every other part of this training, the easier this part is.

My conversations with clients are even more simple now than ever. I look for small ways to connect with them as people so they don't think I'm only about the sale or just getting the gig. Don't fake it. You should really be about knowing them. People buy from people they like. I also let our promo material do as much work as possible for us. That is why we have spent the money and time on great pictures, great promo video, a pro website and more. I don't want to try to sell them on why they should hire us. Bands and artists selling themselves are ineffective anyway. There's a bias there and the buyer has heard it a hundred times. So until you have attracted a quality booking agent, your answer is to let your promo material do the work until word of mouth begins to spread.

We will cover contracts, follow up, agents and detail in the following sections.

# 12. Booking Agents

We've all had dreams of the clouds parting, and in a brilliant bright light, a glorious agent descends from the sky to make all our dreams come true. Sounds wonderful doesn't it? If we could just get someone to book us, we could hit the big time and just focus on our music. There are lots of great agents out there, so you have to ask the question, why would an agent want to book my band?

Let's start by putting ourselves in the agent's shoes. If I'm going to add a band to my roster, I want to make sure of a few things like: Is the band going to be on time? Are they going to sound good? Are they professional? Will they keep a crowd in the room? Are they engaging? Do they properly manage their alcohol consumption? But the bottom line question is going to be, will they make me, the agent, money? This is where past performance equals future success. If a band is doing all the right things that are outlined in this program, an agent will find the band. There's always a chance the band is out there hitting home runs and the agent just hasn't heard about the group yet, but that won't last forever. I'm not saying you can't reach out to them at some point, but for your own benefit, don't do it too early. You have one chance to make a first impression with any agent. You coming off in the slightest bit needy or unprofessional will make it just that much harder when you do have your act together.

Agents get paid anywhere from 10-20% off of the gross amount of each date booked. Again, thinking from the agent point of view, I am going to lean towards groups that tend to be on the higher pay scale already, because I can do the same amount of work for 2-4 times the money. The average dive bar gig at $500 gross is not worth nearly as much to an agent as the event paying 4-5 times or more. The bottom line on this is, if you work to increase your own value, the money will climb with that. When the money climbs, the agents come to you.

As an agent, if I see a great looking press kit and website, with a calendar schedule of solid dates, with a good video promo and great pictures and so on, I get excited about the possibilities. Why, because that band is doing their part to make my job easier. As an agent, I still have to sell the band. It's rare that a client is giving me full reign of their schedule with no input at all. If you give me a package that looks great, sounds great, and you can back it up live, you are doing your part to move to the top of my list.

**Exclusive or non-exclusive** . Alright, so let's say you have it all together, your killing it out there and one day your phone rings. (Choir sings) It's an agent. And have they got a pitch for you. This might be the greatest thing ever or it might be the worst. Why? That depends on who is on the other end of the phone. You must muster up everything you can do to keep your emotions out of this decision. Let me tell you, this is harder than it seems if you have been working towards this your whole life and it feels like the stars just aligned. It's fine to be excited, because after all, they wouldn't have called if you weren't doing well, so let's go ahead and do some proper vetting. If as an artist, you are doing that well, it won't be the last call.
Here are some questions and items to check off before making the decision:

- Call a minimum of 3 other bands the agent works with to ask their experience
- Google the agents name for reviews.
- Is the agent willing to start a non-exclusive relationship until proving themselves?
- If you are working towards exclusivity, what is
cancellation time they are requiring?

- Check out agents' social media. What kind of overall
  tone do they have on it?
- And before you sign anything exclusive, make sure
  to have an attorney look it over.
- And again, be honest with yourself and listen to what your gut is telling you.

I don't want to belabor this too much, but this is one of the big potholes we personally hit. While our experience did have some upsides to it, I have to tell you that we didn't do any of the items above and got ourselves into a situation where we had to go back afterwards and rebuild relationships that had gotten out of sorts by this person. Solid character qualities are a must for this position. Trust will be everything for it to work. Walk in slow and let that develop naturally, while continuing to develop your career, contacts and so on. No one, and I mean no one will ever care about your career more than you. If you are going to turn over the face of your artist career to someone else, make sure that face is a pretty one, metaphorically speaking of course.

# 13. Manager / Road Manager

Like an agent, as a musician, we can glorify the idea of having a manager/road manager as well. So let's look at the facts. First off, what is the difference between a manager and a road manager? A manager is someone who handles all of the business dealing for an artist. A manager is the liaison between agents, venues, sponsors, and more. They can help book radio tours, get sponsors, find attorneys, etc. They are the face of the band and are generally paid 10 - 20% of gross on every show. Many of them will negotiate to get a percentage on merch, sponsorship, and other sources of revenue generated. Managers don't generally travel with the artist unless they are performing the duties of a road manager as well.

Road managers perform all the onsite duties at the venue like coordinating merch set up, hotel rooms, meals, sound and light advancing, and more. Road managers can many times be one of the hired musicians which is a good idea for both parties assuming the musician has good road manager qualities. These qualities include a combination of great people skills along with having the ability to manage details throughout the day.

The above descriptions are very generalized. There is way more to both jobs than I went into here. My hope is that between this section and the agent section, that you started doing some math and realizing how much more you need to make to pay for an agent, manager and road manager. Also, how much more you need to make to attract a quality version of one of these. There are times to add them, but what I hope to prevent is you spending wasted mental energy thinking anyone of these is the key to "take you to the next level"

I used quotes, because that is the most overused phrase when an artist is looking for one of these. The best time to add these roles is when you have so much activity going in either the booking, management or road management area on your own, that you simply can't handle the load. It's a great problem to have and will be an attractive scenario to a good agent/manager.

That being said, if you have a band member that has shown loyalty, is good with people, can manage details and can manage conflict well, this would be a good first step to start delegating out. Start slow or even call it a trial basis to make sure both parties are comfortable with the scenario. Give it a couple months with an easy out for both. Do a low increase in income on the trial so that if it doesn't work out, the band member doesn't feel a huge loss in income and failure. You can even start by asking them to help with a few small road manager duties before even bringing up the job, just to see how they do. Another quote from the book Good to Great, "hire slow, fire fast."

There is one exception to everything above. You've got an artist sugar daddy or you are your own sugar daddy. Money can potentially speed this up, however I would caution turning everything over without a complete knowledge of the business. Again, know one will ever care about your artist career as much as you, no matter how much money you throw at it. The numbers still need to make sense. A good agent, manager and road manager will pay for themselves in a fairly reasonable amount of time. If your goal is to have any one of these, then it's on you to get the business side of your career to the point you will attract a good one.

# 14. Follow UP

There are two types of follow ups we will talk about here. The first being follow-up when working to book a show. The second is the follow up to do after you played the show. Both types provide you with a great opportunity to improve your people skills and no matter who you are, this can be learned. In fact, it's a requirement to advance your career. In either follow up scenario, do your best to listen as much as you talk. Be patient with the conversation and allow it to be fluid. You never know what can come out of follow ups.

**Booking follow up.**

Do your best to **not** make these calls without something additional to add to the conversation other than I just am checking in to see if you want to book my band. Any additional little tidbit can make a difference in the tone of the call. You may need to get creative with this, but here are a few examples. "Hello (name), this is (my name) with the (band/ artist name) do you have a minute?" (If the answer is a no) simply reply, "I apologize, would there be a better time?" If the answer is yes, then say, "I will just be a minute, I am calling to talk about the date we have been discussing, but I also wanted to see if you wanted free tickets to a show we have coming up not far from you?  I can also have a reserved table for you and your guests that night if you are available." It's impossible to play out the rest of these conversations since there are multiple ways it can go and the idea is to let it go where it wants. What you've done here though is show your willingness to give first before asking to get. There are many ways to do this. Get their address to send them some kind of merch like a koozie. Send them a giftcard to some restaurant or coffee shop. As an agent, I had a band slip me a $50 gift card one time after I had already booked them. Guess who I never forgot about? The big point is to set yourself apart by being a giver and not a taker.

What not to do: Do not, and I mean do not make that follow up call about giving reasons to the potential client about why they should book you. First of all, that holds zero credibility when you are talking about your own band. They've heard it all before. Don't be that person. It not only doesn't work, it actually sends the opposite message labeling you as amateur and neediness. Be very conscious of how much time you take on the phone as well. If they want to talk more, let it happen, but if you feel their conversation is rushed and short, simply say, "I know you're busy and I really appreciate the time you've given me." If they haven't come back around by this point to talk about booking you, then throw out almost as an afterthought, "by the way, would you like me to check back with you about booking a date?" There is no amount of forcing the issue that will ever work. They are business owners because they enjoy making their own decisions. This one has to be theirs too. If you are running into a situation where you are just not getting the bookings, the efforts need to be placed on the development sides of this training. Bookings come when you have increased your value.

**After gig follow up.**  This is your opportunity to set the hook for future shows and get referrals for more shows. Again, the whole idea is to give, give, give. Here are some ideas to help with that. Hop on the venue facebook page and give them a gracious thank you. Find there different places online that you can give them reviews and give them a thoughtful accurate review. We printed up some nice thank you notes with our promo picture on to send them. Another gift card to a coffee shop is always a good idea here too. $5 - $10 will go a long way. If you put some thought to this you can come up with some even more creative ways to do this. If you really want to go over the top, gather a little intel and figure out what the clients favorite restaurant is and get a gift card there. Start within your means, but feel free to push the envelope on what you spend on this. Increase your level of giving and your bookings and prices will go up with it.

**Referrals and return bookings**  Ideally you would make this step number two of your post show follow up. Let them feel good about the gift, the good words, the good review and then make the call talk return bookings. The call will be different depending on whether this is a place you would play multiple times in a year or a once a year festival or party. Make sure you thank them for booking you and show your appreciation. When there is a natural break in the conversation say something like, "We get a majority of our private event bookings from referrals. Is there anyone that jumps into your mind that might be a good contact for us?" Then be patient for the response. If they have a name or two for you, ask them permission to use their name when contacting that referral.

At the end of the conversation, almost as an afterthought, ask them if they would like to book a return date as well. That's assuming the client hasn't already brought that up.

# 15. Staying Organized

If you are diligently applying yourself to all of the sections of this program, there will become a time where this section is an absolute necessity. Hopefully sooner than later for you. There are many different ways to stay organized, so if you have a method that works better for you, by all means do that. I will give you what works for me, but what I mostly want you to get is the subjects in which you absolutely need to be organized. I use a CRM (contact relations management), called Less Annoying CRM. I chose this one for a few reasons. It is very simple with only the most basic items. CRMs are designed,  for the most part, CRMs are designed for sales people to keep track of prospects and clients. I didn't sign up to be a sales guy, so the simpler the better. It's also only $10 a month per seat and you only need one seat. Many of them are way over it. This CRM connects with Mailchimp very easily which allows mass communication with multiple people at once separated by groups. For example, I have one group of clients that either wanted to book our band and we weren't available or were interested in our band but they already had the date filled for the year. I can send that group an email all at once out in advance of their next year to remind them of our band. I store every contact from every booking, past booking or potential booking here. I take really good notes for every communication I've had with these people. In sales they call potential clients a pipeline. The more you fill your pipeline, the more gigs you will get. The more gigs you get the less dates you have available. The less dates you have available the more you can charge. Again, it is simple supply and demand and a CRM plays a huge role in that for us. There are more details with more applications that can benefit you in the CRM's video training.

I personally use spreadsheets in google docs to track the money flow for each gig. I set up an estimated expense sheet before the gig and change any numbers I need to after the show. Ex. Band pay, production costs, gas, hotel, reimbursement for expenses either my brother or I have paid for out of our own funds. This helps me figure out how much income we have left over to pay ourselves. I keep all the spreadsheets in one file, but do a different page for each show. There is also a page with running totals of our monthly expenses that I use to track for reimbursements. There are probably better ways to do this, but this one works for me.

**Contracts.** I keep contracts in google docs and just duplicate and edit as needed.  It is important to make sure your outdoor shows either have an indoor option or that there is a **rain or shine clause** stating payment provisions if the show gets rained out. If there is an indoor option, make sure that decisions are made prior to set up. Also make sure to include the hotel rooms and meal details if you've got those worked into the deal. Once you start dipping into higher quality shows, rooms and meals should be included. Some may be ok covering hotel expenses but don't want to mess with booking them. In this case, you can offer them a comparable buyout and take care of it yourself.

If you need double bed rooms, make sure to specify that. The contract should also have a place to specify the amount, due date and how to send the deposit. Usually 20%-50% is acceptable.

Once we fill in the agreement with details connected to a given show, I download the file as pdf. We use a system through Adobe called Echosign. This allows me to upload the pdf that I created and insert signature blocks that can be signed either on the computer or on the phone. Once the process is started it becomes automated sending everybody the agreements in the order you indicated and sending out final copies once all have signed. It even has an automated reminder button to send out daily reminders until completed. I feel it is important to go through this process so that it is super easy for the clients to sign. It is a rare circumstance that we go to any show without a contract. If you try this with physical copies and the mail, you're going to run into issues getting some back. It also gives our clients a feeling of comfort from sheer professionalism of our system. Echosign is $19.99 a month. There are other options you may want to look into. Just remember, if you want paid like a national group, you are going to have to act like one in all areas.

After I send the agreement, I send out an invoice using Quickbooks for the deposit amount with a due date 1 - 2 weeks out. This helps add one more step of professionalism regarding the booking and payment of you or your group.

# 16. Sound and Light Production

I've always been a bit of a geek about this subject. I wouldn't call it my "zone of genius" but it's a solid "zone of excellence." I have always had the mentality of pushing the envelope in production since my first touring band. At a young age, I saw the kind of impact bigger and better production had on our overall presentation of the group. Fortunately, what used to require a 24ft box truck to haul around can now be accomplished with a much smaller trailer. The introduction of high quality powered speakers, digital mixers and LED lighting completely changed the game for indie artists. I'm not going to get into brands or needed watts of power here but more philosophies. In Big Time Grain Co., every time we are able to make advancements in production, we do. Why? Because we know that quality sound and lights turns into quality shows and ultimately quality paychecks. You've probably heard that you can take an average band and make them sound great with good gear and of course a great sound person but an excellent band with bad sound gear and sound tech is never going to sound good. We will discuss crew members in the next chapter.

Our sound philosophy for the amount of gear has been to start with the best quality we can with something that can be expanded as you go. We happen to use the QSC KW and K series, but there are tons of great quality options from EV, JBL, Bose, Mackie and more. Our first QSC rig was good for close to 500 people. As soon as we could, we doubled it which got us up to about 1000 people. In most cases, if you get over 1000 people in your audience, production is provided for those types of shows anyway.

We also use the Behringer X-32 board for mains and monitors. Again, there are many great options, but what we really like from the stage perspective is that we all have individual control of our in-ear monitors from our phones. This makes life much easier if you are in that spot where you have a full time front house engineer, but not to the point of having a monitor tech.

**Lighting:** We are constantly finding ways to improve lighting as well. Fortunately, this is getting more cost effective too. For your front lighting, you are better off having fewer par lights with higher wattage LEDs for easier set up. RGB (red, green, blue) are ok, but RGBWA are better for front with addition of (white and amber) There are lots of creative things to be done with back and mid lighting to create depth and space on the stage. There are creative ways to make your setup unique to you for shows where it is only you and there is no sound company. Upright trussing looks way more pro than black tree stands. Make that move as soon as you can.

**Subbing out.** This is always an option if you can find someone consistently available with the kind of gear you want that fits in your budget. We personally felt like there were too many variables to be limited by whether we take a show or not. Also, over time you end up paying for a complete rig with rental fees and then some.

**Additional ideas:** Fog or preferably haze always help any light show look better, just don't over use. Fog juice will leave nasty residue on your gear where haze is water based and won't. You'll have less crowd and venue complaints with haze too.

Also, use your creativity to stand out. There are so many unique and cool ideas out there to personalize your productions. Making banner support stands out of pvc pipe and then placing 5x5 ft banners on each side of the stage are a nice touch. Use mesh so they are blow-through for outdoor shows and you can fill the pvc with Quikcrete concrete to add weight. Maybe leave your logo unprinted and backlight with a par can so your logo will change color with the lights. The ideas are endless. Pinterest is a good place to look for ideas. Sometimes it's the little, unique and inexpensive ideas that make the biggest impact.

Drum risers have a really big impact. One of the most unique ideas I have seen for that was 5 gallon buckets all held together with a strap, topped with black plywood and a rug. They then used a drape around the sides so you couldn't see the buckets. The best part of that idea was the buckets could all be stacked for travel and between that and the plywood it took up very little room and was really low weight. There are obviously really nice drum stages you can purchase and that would be a good idea eventually. But, don't wait until you can afford it to make improvements when there are other options.

Never stop looking for ways to improve your production and stage. The more pro you come off, the more you can ask.

# 17. The Crew

Just as you don't see national acts showing up, unloading everything by themselves, setting up everything by themselves, running their own merch, etc, so shouldn't you. Now of course you probably won't be able to pull the trigger on all of that up front unless you have someone bankrolling you, but this is the goal to work towards.

**Sound Tech:** This is the first and maybe the most valuable crew move you will make on the front end. Hiring a good sound tech can make all the difference in the world in how a band comes off. It doesn't matter how good of a live sound engineer you are, running it from stage not only isn't as good as having someone out front, but it affects your performance when you are multitasking during a show instead of focusing on being present in the performance.

We made this jump right between that point of being comfortable adding the expense and uncomfortable because our income wasn't quite there. But when we did it, in a very short order our income jumped significantly. I keep a spreadsheet of all the sound techs I know and make sure we are covered for every show. Also, don't forget the earlier lessons of hiring good attitudes as well as talent. Sound techs usually run about $200-$250 per show.

A l**ight tech** was our next jump. In our particular case, I had a son wanting to learn this so we hired him and trained him the way we wanted it done. The power of a great light show with a great performance is icing on the cake. You eventually get to the point in your career where you are working on what we call the last one percent. These are the seemingly small advancements in your career that can make massive differences in how you are received. A lot of groups that are using tracks are preprogramming lights which is a cool way to do it as well. Someone still has to set it all up. As you grow, you want your time to be spent on relationship building and not as your own roadie at your shows. Always work towards that. **Light techs** will be about $100 - $150 on up, per show.

**Stage manager / guitar tech**
This may seem like a luxury item, but when we hired this person, again, we went to another level in our show. First off, there is nothing worse than out of tune instruments. Sure you can stop and tune yourself, but a national act has another guitar brought out to them. Being the guitar player in the band, for me, some of my improvements have to do with the exact right tone for each song, which I accomplish partially with the right guitar for that song. Doing this switch that many times in a show would only work with the help of tech. There are people passionate about this type of work. That is what you are looking for. Every part of our show is mapped out with instrument changes included. This job may start around $100 a show, but increase as they show value and you can. The guy we hired added so much value, we don't want to go to shows without him.

**Merchandise**
This person can also have a major impact on your group. First rule in hiring this person is to make sure they are approachable. Do they smile? Are they easy to talk to? Can you trust them with cash? These people also can be hugely important in future shows if someone in

the crowd has interest in hiring the band. There is a good chance that potential clients will go to the merch booth for info or a card. You also would like to have someone with attention to the appearance of how nice your merch table looks. A merch person will work either on percentage or a guarantee vs a percentage somewhere around 10-20%. Just make it worth their while so they feel valued and enjoy doing it.

Please don't let the totaling of the dollar amounts for these positions discourage you. There is money to make for great gigs that completely justify all four of these positions. Envision these spots being filled with the specific qualities you want in them. The numbers have all worked out for us and we have all four positions filled. You can too.

# 18. Social Media

This might possibly be one of the most fluid topics in the music industry. The way the different platforms change can be daunting to try to keep up with. What we will talk about below are some foundational aspects of how to manage your social media that should pretty much stay the same.

To start with, develop a give, give, give attitude on your platforms. Years ago, a friend taught me how to conduct myself at network meetings.  He said, never talk about your business unless asked. Never give out a business card unless asked. Always ask a lot of questions and figure out how you can help the other person. Do the same thing in social media. If you are constantly posting about shows or trying to get people to buy your music and that is it, then you are over selling and people will quit listening quickly. People want to laugh, be entertained and be inspired. If you do this right, there should be 8-9 posts doing those three things before there is a post asking for something for you or your band. I love Bandsintown for the ease of spreading our calendar around, but I don't engage any of the automatic posting functions for this exact reason. I want to make sure I am not getting out of balance with my give / ask ratios.
Your fans want authenticity. For a long time, people, including myself were apprehensive to put stuff on social media that wasn't perfect. We look at camera angles, facial expressions and so on. I'm not saying you shouldn't pay any attention to those things, but I am saying do it thru the eyes of what exposes the real

you. My brother and I both come out of performance driven backgrounds and so this was somewhat challenging. My brother owns a video company, so this was probably even harder for him because of his years of editing video.

But when he started putting out videos in his house with an unedited iphone video, people loved it and our views and interaction was really great on all of them. Let your fans into your life. When someone sees you perform the first time, they are trying to figure out two things. Do they like you as a person and do they like your music? Your social media, done right, can help with both those before they ever come to a show. Be **YOU** and the right people will follow.

**Consistency**

To help with this, my brother and I have shared a dropbox folder just for this. We are always on the hunt for funny, entertaining or inspiring pictures, videos, boomerangs, etc to put in that dropbox for future use. Post every day and on some platforms multiple times a day. People go through their feeds at different times a day and if they have a ton of friends or follows they may not see yours. Plus, many of the platforms are constantly changing their algorithms and if people are not reacting with your posts, they will probably stop seeing them. Do your best to do periodic google searches on changes made to social media platforms so you can stay current and evolve with them.

If you are running your music business by yourself, it may also be a good idea to start with one at a time and learn to manage it properly rather than spread yourself too thin. If you do that, start with the one your market is most likely to reside in. For example, an older market will be more facebook oriented where the younger market is more Instagram and Snapchat. Twitter seems to cross those lines somewhat. You have to go where your fans are hanging out and reach them there before you ever try to get them to go somewhere different.

**Negativity, stances and sticking to your bran** d.

This is big. Here's what Big Time Grain Co is. We are a country band that loves to play music, have fun, treat people like we want to be treated and do what we love while hopefully inspiring them to pursue their own dreams in the process. Here's what we are not. We are not politicians. We are not an anti this or anti that organization. And this goes for our personal social media as much as our band social media. Think about this for a second. You want to make money doing what you love, correct? Do you not think people "social media stalk" you before they hire you? In an extremely polarized political environment, are you more interested in your opinion than you are getting hired for a job that can help you further your career? Do you want to split your potential gig pool in half for the sake of your opinion. Hopefully you get the point here. Keep the main thing, the main thing.

**Keep learning**

Always do your best to keep learning new ideas on social media. There are tons of cool apps to help make your post fun and interesting. The absolute hilarity that can happen on boomerang alone is worth looking into. Be creative. When something inspires you, capture it and use it to inspire others. Do not and I mean do not tag people in your self promotion post, unless you feel you have too many fans. (that's a joke). Do not group chat people in yourself promotion posts or messages. If they are not annoyed by your first post, they will be when their phone dings every time someone responds. This is not how you build a following .

**Responses:**
Be quick, gracious and authentic with your responses. If someone takes the time to send you a message or comment on something you posted, let them know you saw it and appreciate it.

**Negative Comments:**
If you get a hater on your social media, feel free to delete that comment. You don't need people like that in your circle. Let them take their bad vibes somewhere else. Definitely don't engage.

**Social Media Gurus**
Rick Barker, Taylor Swift's former manager is one of the best out there for teaching proper and effective social media methods and techniques. Rick consults some of the biggest labels as well as talent shows on these subjects and he is accessible to you.

# 19. Email List

This is where the gold is. So many times I hear groups that are communicating to their fans only through social media. Big mistake. Why? As I mentioned earlier, you don't own facebook, twitter or any of them. You have no control over any changes they make. And believe me, they constantly make changes. Sometimes, those changes can make it more difficult to reach your fans. It is a mistake to think that just because you posted something on your social media platform, that all your fans saw it.

What you do have control of is your email list. Your emails may not all get opened every time, but at least you know it got sent to them. Gather emails at shows at your merch booth. Put out sign up cards on the tables. Give incentive to sign up, like a drawing of a merch item that night. Ask people from stage to sign up so you can stay in touch and get to know them.

When you send out emails, use the same principle of give 9 times before you ask once. Ideas for giving can be a lot around giving people the opportunity to learn more about you as a person and an artist. Rick Barker also has a lot of additional info on this subject.

# 20. Conclusion

We greatly appreciate you and your dedication to your music career. You obviously care or you wouldn't have made it this far in the book. Let me challenge you to forever be a student.

Never stop learning.  Growth in all areas of your life is the key to an ultimate fulfilling life, whether we are talking about music or just life in general.  If you received this book, that means you are signed up on our email list.  We will continue to produce and send you content to help you with your career.  Don't hesitate to send us emails with questions you may have.  Your questions help us identify more areas that may need to be covered.  May your music career be everything you dreamed of and then some.  You got this!!!

**Additional Resources:**
Play Music Make More Online Course
https://www.playmusicmakemore.com/online-course
Play Music Make More Music Biz Mastermind Group
https://www.playmusicmakemore.com/Music%20Business%20Mastermind
Play Music Make More Blog
https://www.playmusicmakemore.com/blog
Dream Big Series Podcast
https://linktr.ee/dreambigseries
Sign up for our email list and continue to get valuable additional tips on building your successful music career.
https://www.playmusicmakemore.com/e-book